50 STOCK INVESTMENT RULES FOR BEGINNERS

THE COLLECTIVE INSIGHTS OF 25 INVESTING EXPERTS

RANDALL STEWART

THE STEWART EDGE PUBLISHING

CONTENTS

DISCLAIMER

As stipulated by law, I cannot and do not make any guarantees about your ability to get results or earn any money from the ideas, information, tools or strategies presented.

The risk of loss in trading securities and options can be substantial. Please consider all relevant risk factors, including your own personal financial situation, before investing or trading. Stocks and options do involve risk and are not suitable for all investors.

Use caution and always consult your accountant, lawyer or professional advisor before acting on this or any information related to a lifestyle change or your finances.

Past results of any individual trader or trading system published by the author are not indicative of future returns by that trader or system and are not indicative of future returns which may be realized by you.

All strategies and examples are provided for informational and educational purposes only and should not be construed as investment advice under any circumstances. Such set-ups are not solicitations of any order to buy or sell a financial security.

Any financial numbers referenced here should not be considered average earnings, exact earnings or promises for actual or future performance.

STOCK INVESTING TOOL KIT

How to Get $29 Worth of Investment Research
for Free

To get your bonuses, go to:

http://tiny.cc/stock-investing

Free Bonus #1: Top 5 Current Stock Market Trends.

Tap into 5 industries poised to show consistent growth over the next two years. Take advantage of changes in the economic climate that'll fuel rapid growth in certain sectors.

Free Bonus #2: Growth Investing using the C.A.N.S.L.I.M. Approach.

Find market leaders using the key insights from the C.A.N.S.L.I.M. approach to growth investing. Quickly implement the main strategies summarized in this special report.

Free Bonus #3: Momentum Stock Investing Guidelines.

Guide your decision-making with a series of actionable rules and a trading routine that'll allow you to increase your probability of coming out on top. Learn how to optimize your returns in fast-growing stocks.

To receive your stock investing tool kit and discover how to capture the upside momentum of fast-growing market leaders, go to:

http://tiny.cc/stock-investing

INTRODUCTION

As far as I'm concerned there are only two types of people in this world: those who already know a heck-of-a-lot about stock investing and those who could learn more. Stock investing has been a great means to build personal wealth over the past century and will continue to do so for some time to come.

However, investing blindly without a set of pre-defined rules is a recipe for disaster. It would be about as difficult as swimming upstream in Jell-O. Without rules to guide your decision-making you default to investing using a hope-based model - hope the heck your stock pick works out.

What you're about to discover are some of the most effective, time-tested rules you should consider integrating into your arsenal of stock investing strategies and approaches that'll make a material difference to your investment portfolio. Without establishing pre-defined investment rules, your chances of ongoing success are about as good as nailing a blob of mercury to the wall.

This guide showcases the sage advice offered by over two dozen reputable investment educators. Their rules have allowed them and others to generate consistent returns despite what the markets might be doing. This quick read will provide you with 50 concrete stock investing rules that'll save you time and a bottle of Tylenol trying to figure everything out on your own.

Rules - Guidelines - Tips?

But before we look at each of these rules, let me share a quick word about the term "rules". Whether we're talking about investment rules, guidelines or tips, these terms can be used interchangeably in the context of following an investment approach that'll both preserve and grow your capital over time.

The term "rule" may be a more fitting description for the purpose of this resource, which is to allow you to grow your capital using various stock investment approaches. However, in many cases you could also use the terms guidelines and tips to describe the underlying concept.

The intent of this quick action guide is to provide you with those key concepts and appropriate rules that'll serve you well in most typical stock investment decisions. Out of the hundreds of stock investment rules to choose from, I've selected those rules that most novice investors entering the investment landscape today would benefit from.

You'll find that this guide, walks you through a series of rules applicable to various aspects of the investment process, from saving to invest to placing your trades with greater resolve. Use those rules you feel would best serve your particular investment philosophy and set aside the ones that don't turn your crank.

Investing is a personal journey. There is no "be all - end all" magic formula to follow. I hope you're chomping at the bit to get started. Ready to explore what approaches and key investment concepts resonate with you the most?

The Most Common Investment Approaches:

Before we do a deep dive into the rules, let's first lay out the foundation upon which we'll build the various rules for specific circumstances.

The first concept we'll need to address is defining some of the key investment approaches you can follow. There are three of note you should be aware of:

1. Value Investing,
2. Income Investing, and
3. Growth Investing.

Each of these basic approaches taps into specific benefits and challenges. Therefore, it's important to adopt a set of rules or criteria as to how to best profit from each approach.

Fortunately, these three approaches are not mutually exclusive of each other. In other words, you could theoretically use all three approaches in your investment portfolio for the various positions you're holding. As you're about to see, the concept of diversifying risk can be achieved by adopting several different rules. Let's explore these three investment approaches right now.

1. Value Investing:

As the name implies, value investing looks at purchasing shares in businesses that are trading below their fair market price. The objective is then to hold onto the stock until it can be sold at a profit above its true intrinsic value.

This approach focuses on ensuring that the investor purchases the shares of stock with a margin of safety so as to preserve capital and limit loss. Often these investors look for mispricing in the stock market whereby they can buy the stock at 30% or more below the estimated intrinsic value or retail price.

Investors typically select businesses with solid fundamentals in the areas of debt levels, book value and return on invested capital over a 5 to 10-year period of analysis.

Using a value investing approach requires discipline and patience since the holding period can be in excess of 5 years. For many value investing is about as exciting as eating steamed broccoli or watching cement cure in a parking lot. Investors with a low risk tolerance and a lengthy time horizon often gravitate towards this approach to investing in the markets.

In a nutshell, a patient value investor holding onto a fundamentally solid company expects the stock price to move from being undervalued by Mr. Market to eventually overvalued, at which point it is sold. It's like opening a bottle of ketchup, you've got to wait awhile before anything comes out. But, when it does, watch out.

2. Income Investing:

An income investing approach attempts to create a regular stream of income from quarterly or annual dividend payments. Mature companies that have a long solid track record will often reward investors with a portion of the company's profits being returned as a cash dividend.

An income investor is looking for mature businesses with consistent levels of earnings, sales and cash flow that entices shareholders with dividend payments. Mature businesses are those that have reached national or international status as a global leader having finished their growth spurt and expansion into the global economy.

Often income investors are looking for companies that have historically paid good dividends for periods of time in excess of 10 years. These investors usually have a long-term holding period and often desire holding onto companies that offer a low investment risk with income generation being used to fund retirement or other major expenses, like a college education or a home.

Investors also like to hold onto businesses that are not significantly affected by economic cycles. In other words, they focus on owning companies with a track record of consistently paying out dividends no matter what the economy is doing.

3. Growth Investing:

Growth investing focuses on purchasing shares in businesses that are experiencing higher than market average earnings growth. This could be due to an increase in market share across the globe, the introduction of new technologies or innovations that are in demand or new market trends.

Growth investors seek out businesses that are in their infancy of their growth phase with the potential to grow and become stable mature companies down the road. In the meantime, these investors, who often have a shorter holding period of less than 5 years, focus on stock price appreciation in those companies experiencing a major positive change in their industry.

These investors tend to select businesses that have superior growth in sales, earnings and invested capital. With an increased probability of rapid stock price appreciation comes a higher level of risk tolerance needed. If you desire earning greater than average returns, you must be willing to assume greater than average market risk. Growth investors often profit best from younger regional companies experiencing rapid growth in earnings and invested capital compared to the market averages as these businesses expand nationwide.

What's important to realize is that all three classic approaches to stock investing have their place in any investor's portfolio, whether you're just starting out or at the end of your career as an active investor.

Your Primary Investment Objectives:

Whether you're investing in the stock market, real estate, commodities or systematized businesses, an underlying theme permeates throughout each investment vehicle. No matter which vehicle you choose to invest in, your overall investment objective must take into account three key factors, namely:

1. Protecting your initial capital.
2. Factoring in upside growth potential.
3. Generating multiple sources of growth.

Ideally, when investing in the stock market, you want to build in a margin of safety for each of your stock positions. You don't want to lose money the way a balloon loses air. Creating a margin of safety can be accomplished in a couple of ways.

The most obvious is by purchasing shares of the stock or the equity in question below the fair market value assessed for that holding. Online resources like Morningstar do much of the heavy lifting in making these assessments. And many online discount brokers provide these reports free of charge.

You should also note that a difference always exists between the price you and the market is willing to pay for the shares of stock and the true intrinsic value the company has. One is based on the whim of the market. The other is derived from key fundamental metrics used to assess the assets, liabilities, revenue and expenses the business or entity has.

Purchasing shares of stock when Mr. Market has undervalued the price of the holding builds in a margin of safety. Over time stock prices trend towards what the fair market value of the holding is, whether the price in the market is under or overvalued. Buying shares below the fair market value allows you upside growth potential and minimizes capital loss. This is what the "pure" value investor seeks.

The second way you can build in some downside protection of your stock's price is by selling covered calls on those equities you own, which also trade in the options market.

Similar to a property owner getting monthly rent for his or her property, option contracts can be sold to generate an income stream. The sale of option contracts for stock holdings you own puts money immediately into your brokerage account. It's like that monthly rental check that you might deposit at the beginning of the month from a tenant.

In doing so, that cash injection reduces your cash basis for your stock holding. Having cash being deposited into your brokerage account reduces your overall purchase price for that holding.

Which brings us to key factor #2, the upside growth potential of your investment. All successful stock investors use a combination of metrics and insights for assessing the upside growth potential of a business. As you're about to see in this guide, most look at certain business fundamentals like the revenue growth rate, debt-to-equity ratio or earnings per share growth rate to help assess business sustainability.

They take in consideration whether or not the business will benefit from some sort of economic advantage that their competition doesn't have. This could be things like patented technologies, economies of scale, massive brand appeal or monopolistic control of a specific industry.

And they also factor in what type of management

team is running the business. Management that looks out for shareholder interests, as opposed to sucking the company dry with outrageous salaries and bonuses, provides investors with a certain degree of confidence the company will be around in 30 years.

The fundamentals of a business, the economic advantage it commands, and how the management team treats the business and shareholders, influences the upside growth potential you might experience for any stock holding. Being mindful of them and following rules that foster positive growth is paramount to your success.

Finally, all investors should strive to develop multiple sources of growth. The most obvious is through stock price appreciation whereby you see the stock's price rise gradually over time as the business's fundamentals improve. But there are also two other sources you should keep in mind and they are dividends and options.

Mature, well-established companies often reward their shareholders by paying out a portion of their earnings in the form of cash dividends. Quarterly dividends deposited into your brokerage account can accumulate over time growing your initial investment capital.

As briefly mentioned, selling monthly option contracts on stock positions you already own can generate a significant annual return in addition to capital appreciation. This conservative investment strategy can generate double digit annual returns once you understand the basics. It's something worth considering exploring down the road.

To recap, all experienced stock investors look for ways of protecting their capital while creating upside growth potential from multiple sources with their holdings.

Where Should You Park Your Money?

Depending on who you're listening to, you'll receive conflicting advice as to how you should invest and where you should park your money. Most of the top stock investment educators showcased in this resource tend to fall into the category of do-it-yourself advocates. This means that they'll often advocate buying and selling individual stocks and options, along with the occasional exchange traded fund or ETF.

An assumption I'm going to make is that you've selected this particular guide to help you become a better do-it-yourself stock investor. With this in mind, most of the investment rules reflect this mindset and overall philosophical approach to investing. Let's take a look at your first chapter that of saving to invest right now.

SAVING TO INVEST

The rules outlined in this initial chapter tend to focus on meeting the basic needs of most novice investors just learning the ropes. The tips provided assume that you'll initially have a more passive approach to managing your investments as you learn. As your investment knowledge grows, you'll be in a better position to actively seek higher overall returns, which we'll cover in greater detail in some of the other chapters. Let's first explore those rules you'll want to adopt to get the ball rolling.

Personal finance and small business author, Laura Adams suggests following three specific investment rules when initially getting started. They serve as a strong reminder for even the seasoned investor. The first rule of thumb to take into consideration is:

1. Clarify the purpose of your money.

Most people have a fixed amount of income coming into the household. If you're like the majority of income-earners in the workforce, most of those funds will go towards the necessities of life. Paramount to your success as an investor is gaining peace of mind with your financial affairs by first setting aside some of your savings for unforeseen circumstances.

As Paul Mladjenovic says in "Stock Investing for Dummies":

"Make sure you have an emergency fund."

Economist Burton Malkiel, author of "A Random Walk Down Wall Street", also supports the notion of creating a sense of security in managing your financial affairs by having a "rainy day" fund. Before you can allocate specific funds for investment purposes for your "sunny day" fund, it's important to set aside a portion for any unforeseen emergency.

And how much should you try to set aside? A reasonable goal advocated by many financial advisors is to have 3 months' worth of net income in some sort of savings vehicle that 'll provide you with quick access in case of an emergency.

As well, no matter where you are at in your investment journey, it's important to establish a base level of how much you possess in terms of tangible assets like real estate holdings, chattels, insurance, cash savings, etc. List your assets in decreasing order of liquidity. Doing so, enables you to see how much cash you can generate for both "rainy" and "sunny" day situations.

Along with your outstanding short-term consumer and credit card debt, take a look at any long-term debt obligations like a mortgage or vehicle loan. Again, list these liabilities based on when the debt obligation comes due. The bottom line of this little exercise is to determine what you need to track. A key concept of any successful financial plan is:

"What you can track, you can control."

The second rule Laura Adams is a big proponent of is:

2. *Know the difference between saving and investing.*

Fundamental to any investment approach is systematically allocating capital for investment purposes. Saving is an accumulative process that takes your hard-earned dollars and systematically sets a portion aside for future investments. Saving is putting money aside so that it is exposed to little or no risk of capital loss.

Investing is the process of moving those accumulated savings into vehicles that will grow those funds through capital appreciation. This appreciation can occur through upward price movements of the underlying asset or through income generation. Investing almost always involves a higher degree of risk than saving. However, the smart investor knows how to reduce or eliminate risk from capital loss by following pre-defined rules.

In order to invest, you need to have the discipline to set aside savings for investment purposes. If you do not target funds for investing you cannot invest. If you cannot invest, you cannot expect to achieve your financial goals and dreams any time soon. As economist Burton Malkiel says:

"Start saving now, not later."

He goes on to say:

"Trust in time, rather than timing. The secret to getting rich slowly (but surely) is the miracle of compound interest."

Michael Katchen, the CEO of Wealthsimple, also advocates to start saving as early as possible, even if it's only a small amount each month in the beginning. This sentiment is echoed by most well-known financial educators.

MJ DeMarco, author of "The Millionaire Fastlane", points out that:

"Wealth is a process, not an event."

By getting into the habit of committing a small portion of your income for both "rainy" and "sunny" day saving, the entire investment process becomes less daunting. Unlike most Americans who wait too late until they begin saving and investing for retirement, you'll be in the enviable position of being at peace with the process. With a longer time horizon, more lucrative investment opportunities are sure to present themselves.

DeMarco recommends that one should:

> *"Live below your means with the intent to expand your means."*

When you dial back your expenses and focus on creating wealth through investments, you increase the probability of reaching your financial objectives sooner than later. Delaying self-gratification in the short term can lead to achieving financial freedom decades earlier. This is due to what Albert Einstein calls the 8th wonder of the world: compound interest.

For the average investor, saving typically involves, depositing and stockpiling cash in a bank account. You have immediate access to your cash in exchange for a low rate of return from any interest gains you might accumulate over time.

Whereas, investing requires that you commit your savings to an investment vehicle that'll provide a significant degree of capital appreciation over time. Setting aside money for long-term investment purposes requires that you implement a couple of strategies in order to increase the probability of coming out on top, namely:

1. Patience.
2. Perseverance.

Investing will try your patience over time. You may be tempted to "re-allocate" investment funds to pay for that well-deserved vacation you've been dreaming about or that state of the art industrial strength espresso machine that also bakes baguettes.

We live in a society that is heavily influenced by marketing efforts promoting immediate self-gratification. It's challenging to stay the course, given this constant bombardment by the media. However, it's well worth the effort to stay the course. Who knows? Maybe in 20 years you'll be in the enviable position to take that dream vacation and buy that handy dandy machine when you've reached a point of financial freedom with your investments. It all starts with a bit of patience.

You'll also need to stay the course despite what is happening with the world economy. All markets do not trend upward in a perfectly straight line. They tend to snake up to higher and higher levels experiencing short periods of downward instability. These temporary setbacks will try your patience. This is where perseverance comes in. Know that by sticking to a consistent investment plan, you will build your wealth over time.

The third tidbit of advice that Laura Adams advocates is to:

3. Use tax-advantaged accounts for faster results.

Several retirement accounts like the 401(k), 403(b) and simple IRA help you build wealth and cut your tax bill at the same time. These traditional accounts defer taxation until retirement. One of the biggest advantages of a workplace 401(k) is that the company may offer to match your retirement contributions up to a set limit. This is free money, if you're in the enviable position of working for such a company.

One of my favorite tax-advantaged accounts is the Roth IRA [TFSA in Canada], which any 18-year old with a U.S. social security number and U.S. mailing address can open. Pre-taxed contributions can grow from within the account to be withdrawn tax-free in the future. Every young investor should consider opening a Roth IRA account because of the flexibility it offers and tax-saving benefits into the future.

Investment author and blogger Catherine Brock suggests that newbie investors:

"Work the tax perks."

She suggests that if your current employer doesn't offer a 401(k), then max out your contributions in either a traditional or Roth IRA, which amounts to $6000 in 2021. The added incentive is that if you're 50 or older, you're allowed an additional $1000 contribution room in IRA's.

Which brings us to the subject of what to initially place in your investment accounts. Both Warren Buffett, the Oracle of Omaha and John Bogle, the father of Index Investing, are on the same page when offering advice to novice investors. They both feel that you should own the entire stock market or major portion thereof, which brings us to the next rule.

4. Low-cost index funds are sensible for most novice investors.

What both of these investment gurus are saying is that by mirroring the performance of a portion of your investment portfolio with that of a broad index like the S&P 500, you mitigate risk through diversification.

By investing in a broad U.S. based index through a low-cost index fund you also account for any detrimental effects of fees eroding your capital appreciation. Many actively managed funds charge excessive fees that eat away at returns and dividend income.

Buffett suggests considering using the passive strategy of investing in low-cost, broad-based index funds if you're not concerned about generating stable dividend income.

Index funds have historically produced overall returns that are slightly less than what the actual markets are returning on an annual basis. Historically, the S&P 500 has generated an average return of approximately 10% when looking at a long time horizon of 80 to 90 years. This longer time horizon takes into account both major stock market corrections and positive up trending bull markets that impact overall returns.

It makes sense to allocate a portion of your stock investment portfolio to an Index fund that'll provide you with passive growth down the road.

Piggybacking off of this rule is to look at investing as an ongoing process. By making systematic investments in the stock market, you're able to take advantage of both timing opportunities and capital appreciation of your savings, which is summarized in the next rule.

5. Invest consistently in the stock market.

Both blogger Catherine Brock and Charles Carlson, the author of "Big Safe Dividends", feel that novice investors should invest a consistent amount of money each month. This enables you to take advantage of time diversification, thus reducing your overall investment risk. By spreading investments over time, you limit the risk of purchasing shares when the markets may be over-priced.

This is sound advice for anyone starting out, since it's a methodical approach that ensures you're continually building your portfolio over time. Automatic contributions to a 401(k) [or RRSP in Canada] can be so useful for the goal of retirement saving, which typically has a longer time horizon.

However, as your financial education increases and you become more adept at understanding how the markets work, you may wish to follow the approach of many top-notch investors and allocate capital when the markets experience a slight pullback.

This approach requires that you adopt some specific rules or safeguards to move into the markets with a degree of confidence and high probability of success. We'll address this situation in an upcoming chapter.

Finally, as you begin to identify winning positions in your stock portfolio, look at consolidating these positions over time by periodically picking up additional shares of stock. Buy more shares of high-quality stocks at reasonable prices. Avoid the notion of looking for untested new opportunities that may or may not pan out. You want to focus on propping up your winners.

Not only do you need to consider investing on a

regular basis, but you also should also follow John Bogle's advice.

6. Stay the course with your Index fund(s).

As a long-term investor, you must have the discipline to not only invest on a regular basis but also stay invested in the markets with that portion of your portfolio allocated to index funds.

Index funds offer some great advantages for the investor just starting out, namely:

1. High returns when held long-term as a passive investment.
2. Low portfolio management fees since these funds are not actively managed.
3. Lower tax liabilities when held long-term and/or in tax exempt accounts.
4. Lower risk of errors and blunders, especially when starting out.
5. Lower levels of anxiety about errors and blunders.

Even though the market may present itself as being risky in the short-term, you're better off waiting patiently than trying to move into and out of the markets with these funds. Markets over the past 100 years have historically trended upwards. Realizing that you have a longer time horizon for growth to occur should be reassuring. I should note that this specific rule applies to those individuals who have a portion of their investment portfolio allocated to an Index fund, as opposed to individual stocks.

In contrast to these buy and hold passive investors like John Bogle and Burton Malkiel, are those who are actively involved in managing their holdings. Investment educators who advocate a do-it-yourself approach, feel that with some stock investment knowledge you can out-perform average market returns. They often invest in individual stocks as opposed to broad market indexes as their primary investment strategy. Here are three rules to keep in mind as you gain confidence in your investment prowess.

7. Do your stock homework on your holdings.

TV personality and investor James Cramer emphasizes that one should investigate before investing. Be a stock market detective. Cramer is all about establishing pre-defined rules to keep the do-it-yourself investor out of trouble. Part of the investment process needs to be analyzing the profitability of any business for which you're considering purchasing shares.

Just like doing homework at school better prepares you for passing a test, so does investigating a business's viability and sustainability. This notion factors into your success as an investor.

As your stock portfolio expands, you'll want to devote more time to monitoring your individual holdings. The simple habit of spending 10 to 20 minutes a day looking at your individual stock positions can go a long way in keeping you out of trouble.

Fidelity's Magellan Fund legend Peter Lynch, author of "Beating the Street", also agrees with Cramer. He feels that the person who turns over the most rocks wins the game when it comes to finding solid companies. Lynch feels that you should:

> *"Never invest in any company before you've done the homework on the company's earnings prospects,*

financial condition, competitive position, plans for expansion, and so forth."

We'll address each of these major decision-making factors as we explore the various investment approaches you may wish to undertake. What's encouraging are the comments about investing made by Warren Buffett. He says:

"You don't need to be a rocket scientist. Investing is not a game where the guy with the 160 IQ beats the guy with the 130 IQ."

In other words, it doesn't take a genius to learn the basics of stock investing. However, what will try your patience and affect your performance, are the behavioral mistakes you'll make as you learn how to follow sound investment rules. This is why a whole chapter on the mental game of stock investing is included in this guide.

Start by adopting those investment strategies that focus on both capital preservation and reasonable growth. When you start looking into individual stock holdings keep this foremost in your mind.

8. Diversify your stock holdings across several sectors to control risk.

James Cramer has been big on both selecting just a handful of individual stocks to keep track of once you're more confident in your investment abilities and diversifying those holdings across several economic sectors.

All businesses represented in the stock market have been loosely grouped into common industries, which are a part of 11 economic sectors. Examples of economic sectors are consumer staples, energy, financials, technology and health care. What James Cramer and investment author Phil Town, author of "Rule #1" and "Payback Time", advocate is that you spread out your positions across several unrelated sectors.

Cramer goes on to say that no more than 20% of your total investment portfolio should be concentrated in any one sector. He feels that by diversifying your holdings you can reduce risk. Shifts in market sentiment can make one sector more attractive than another. Spreading out your positions helps to keep your overall returns more consistent.

9. Practice paper trading if you invest in individual stocks.

In keeping with Phil Town's investment philosophy of not losing money, he strongly recommends that novice investors develop the necessary skills as a do-it-yourself actively engaged investor by paper trading.

Paper trading is a dry run of the actual investment process with one exception. No actual money is exchanged when buying and selling securities. Many online discount brokers offer paper trading platforms that allow you to trade free of charge, keeping track of your profits and losses while you learn. This is a great approach to start with as it allows you to discover:

- how to enter and exit the market.
- how to build a balanced portfolio.
- how to sell (and buy) covered calls on stock you own.
- how to deal with market sentiments.

Town suggests you should practice paper trading for at least a month and preferably for a couple of months before committing any of your hard-earned money. He says that the markets aren't going anywhere. Great investment opportunities present themselves in the stock market every week. By paper trading you build confidence, skills and strategies that'll serve you well moving forward.

Do not confuse familiarity with an investment approach or system with knowledge and understanding. It is only through experience that you're able to build the wisdom to reach your full potential as an investor. Take the time to paper trade in the beginning, so you can learn from your mistakes, your feelings and what it takes to be more successful.

2

VALUE INVESTING

Many novice investors look to value investing as an investment approach to follow after they've invested in an initial exchange-traded fund or ETF. As previously mentioned, holding onto a broad-based index fund like the S&P 500 allows you to invest passively for the long haul.

When you get to the point where you're ready to explore the wonderful world of individual stocks, many consider using a value investing approach. Value investing focuses on buying undervalued solid companies when Mr. Market prices them below their fair market value. A value investor is able to pick up the holding with a margin of safety, thus making it more challenging to lose money on the transaction. Here are eight rules to help you with this investment approach.

1. When you buy a stock, plan to hold it forever.

Warren Buffett has a reputation of being a value investor foremost. His ideal stock pick enables his holding company Berkshire Hathaway to hold onto the stock for decades to come. He's looking for businesses with a long, solid, track record of appreciating stock price and the potential to continue to do so for years to come.

Value investors need to be patient with the process as it may take years for the stock price to climb back up to its true intrinsic value. Investment author Steve Smith believes:

> "The longer your holding period, the higher your odds of success."

He explains that on any given day in the markets your probability of generating a positive return is just above 53%. Not much better than the flip of a coin. However, extend that time period out one year and your odds of success leap to 74%. Now, should you look at a 20-year holding period, you would find that no negative returns have been reported in the U.S. equity markets. As Sponge Bob Square Pants says:

"That's pretty impressive all right."

2. *Take into consideration the historical lows for the stock's price before buying.*

American value investor Walter Schloss suggests that when you buy a deep value stock, try to buy at the low of the past few years. What he means by this is that if a stock drops in price from $100 to $60, you may find this to be an acceptable, attractive entry point, yet be potentially problematic. For example, what if the stock price was $30 just a couple of years prior to this, your decision to buy at $60 could expose you to vulnerability.

Begin by trying to find value-oriented stocks that are trading at the low end of their historical range. When using a value investing approach, you'll want to look at long-term historical trends for the stock, focusing on those stocks with a narrow historical range. This means analyzing price changes on a technical chart of the stock over periods of years. This'll give you a better sense of where the stock price has been and where it may head.

Looking at historical trends of price, dividend payouts, equity growth and sales growth gives you a better feel for what the business is capable of producing moving forward. As a value investor, you want to see conservative growth potential for years to come.

3. Know the difference between price and value.

Both Warren Buffett and his No. 1 man, Charlie Munger, emphasize adhering to this rule no matter what type of investor you are. Price is what Mr. Market is willing to sell you shares in a business at. It's based on the current sentiment in the market, which is in effect a popularity contest. Businesses go into and out of favor with Mr. Market all the time.

Value is often expressed as the amount of money the business would be worth should all of its assets be sold. Warren Buffett points out that:

"Price is what you pay. Value is what you get."

Value investors are constantly looking for mispricing in the stock market. Often fundamentally solid businesses with a solid track record of generating equity and revenue year over year can experience a temporary disconnect between stock price and value when a market correction happens.

For example, during a recessionary period many companies actually strengthen their competitive advantage and emerge from the downturn with a leaner and meaner version of the business. These businesses have the potential to surprise on the upside when the stock is purchased at a discount and held long-term.

Smart value investors look for this mispricing in the market where there is a disconnect between price and value. Concentrate your efforts on high quality companies trading at reasonable prices.

James Cramer so succinctly puts it. He says:

> *"Buy damaged stocks, not damaged companies."*

A fundamentally sound company that has been recently treated unfairly in the stock market should not be confused with one that is losing market share and sustainability as a business model.

4. Better to buy assets at a discount than to buy earnings.

The father of value investing, Ben Graham has always touted that it's easier to find deep value stocks in a company that has tangible assets than to base your decision on future earnings potential. Earnings can change dramatically in the short-term, especially if the business doesn't have some sort of competitive advantage that'll set it apart from its competition.

Assets typically change slowly over time. So, the prudent value investor looks to picking up those deep discount stocks and hopes that some catalyst will cause the stock price to move closer to its true intrinsic value.

5. Never invest in a business you cannot understand.

When you move beyond the realm of investing in passively managed ETF's and into the world of selecting individual stock picks, avoid the mistake of getting involved in overly complex business models. Avoid complicated businesses in the beginning when you're just starting out as an investor. Not to say that at some point down the road you could consider exploring more involved businesses.

One way to do this is to follow the advice of investment gurus like Phil Town and Peter Lynch.

"Invest in what you know, and nothing more."

Peter Lynch suggest that you aim to be very familiar with the companies and industries in which you invest. He goes on to say that:

"If you're prepared to invest in a company, then you ought to be able to explain why in simple language that a fifth grader could understand, and quickly enough so the fifth grader won't get bored."

Which brings us to one of Phil Town's rules for success, namely:

6. Buy wonderful stocks based on four success factors.

Town is famous for his No. 1 stock investing rule: Don't lose money. This rule is based on four success factors:

1. Meaning.
2. Moat.
3. Margin of safety.
4. Management.

Let's explore each in greater detail, starting with "meaning". Most individual stock pickers recommend researching those businesses that have some sort of personal meaning to you. The argument is that if you have a personal connection to the business or what it promotes, you'll be more motivated to do the initial research and try to understand how the business makes its money.

The second factor "moat" refers to the company's competitive advantage in the marketplace. What is it that keeps other competitor's from entering and dominating the market? Is it a proprietary innovation, economies of scale, easily recognized brand or other advantage that creates a well-defended moat around the castle?

A wide moat is established when a business has solid fundamentals. It shows up in metrics such as the return on invested capital, earnings per share growth rate, equity growth rate and sales growth rate being above 10% every year. More on this in a moment.

The third factor "margin of safety" shows up in how much on sale the business is in comparison to its true intrinsic value. The true intrinsic value of a business can be assessed by looking at the growth rates mentioned along with debt levels to arrive at an estimated value.

The fourth factor Town uses in his assessment is "management". The management team needs to be trustworthy and focus on the shareholder's interests, not their personal wealth. Are they being paid outrageous salaries, bonuses and incentives that drain corporate assets from the coffers?

By keeping these four factors in mind, when assessing the potential of any stock holding, you'll be in a better position to pick winners.

When is comes to selecting potential stock picks, most investors focus on just a handful of fundamental indicators. Covered call educator Michael Thomsett, the author of "Options Trading for the Conservative Investor", suggests following the following simple rule to keep the whole analysis process manageable.

7. Combine a very short list of key indicators for stock selection.

As William Priest Jr., the Managing Director at BEA Associates, says:

> *"Financial statements are like a bikini. What they reveal is interesting. What they conceal is vital."*

Most do-it-yourself stock investors who write about the subject advocate tracking less than 10 parameters when assessing business quality. Given that you'll not only use these metrics to select but also monitor your holdings, it makes sense to keep the list of parameters down to just a handful.

Besides focusing your attention on just a handful of metrics you also want to use those that track the rate of growth. Raw numbers won't help you much in assessing the growth potential of any business. It's the year over year rate of change that provides you with the assessment knowledge that'll make your investment decisions easier. Rate of change, whether negative or positive, gives you a better sense of how the business is performing.

As to which indicators to use, this varies from one guru to the next. Some of the more popular parameters to track are:

- Return on Invested Capital.
- Sales Growth Rate.
- Earnings Per Share Growth Rate.
- Book Value Per Share Growth Rate.
- Free Cash Flow Growth rate.
- Debt to Equity Ratio.
- Earnings to Price Yield.
- Price to Sales Ratio.
- PEG Ratio.
- Payout Ratio for Dividends

Thomsett also suggests following this basic rule:

8. Avoid companies that have never reported a profit, or whose stock price has been falling over many years.

Once again, as a value investor you want to see the financials for businesses over the long haul. By focusing only on those businesses with a proven, long-term track record, you're in a more powerful position to profit from your selections. Companies new to the market that have yet to report a net profit do not make good value investments. Nor do those companies with a track record of losing market share and profits over several years. Trying to make money from businesses in a downward spiral is like trying to teach an elephant to tap dance on a bar stool.

3

INCOME INVESTING

Most businesses that make excellent candidates for value investing are also strong considerations for an income investing approach to stock investing. As businesses expand their reach across the globe, growth begins to slow down. In order for these multi-national companies to maintain shareholder interest they often reward long-term investors with dividends. Such companies are confident their future profitability will support a dividend payment; thus, they're inclined to return some of those profits back to the shareholders. This is where an income investing approach comes into the mix.

Income investors typically look for a regular stream of cash being deposited into their brokerage accounts either from dividend payments and/or option premiums. Let's address several rules to consider following for dividends before exploring options income from stocks you own.

Dividend Investing Rules:

Charles Carlson in his book "The Little Book of Big Dividends" follows four key factors as they apply to dividends. He also divides the universe of dividend investing into two segments, namely income and growth.

Being well-established, mature businesses, "Income" dividend companies tend to return more of the profits back into the pockets of the shareholders. "Growth" dividend companies tend to be younger. They usually still have high profitability levels and feel they can return a smaller portion of their profits back to the shareholders in the form of a dividend while still funding capital expansion projects.

Let's look at four rules for consideration based on Carlson's four key factors.

1. Choose growth dividend companies with a payout ratio of 30 to 40% and income dividend companies between 50 and 70%.

The payout ratio is the percentage of the company's net earnings paid out to investors as dividends. A lower ratio provides a safer source of income for you.

Growth companies tend to hold onto revenue to fund future growth whereas income companies like to reward investors with higher payouts. You'll want to avoid ratios between 70 and 100% as these levels may be unsustainable resulting in the dividend being cut or eliminated altogether.

2. Choose dividend stocks that have attractive total-return potential, not just dividend return.

The dividend return or yield is the percentage of the share's stock price that you get back every year from dividend payments. It's calculated by dividing the stock's annual dividend yield by its share price to give you a rate of return that is typically expressed as a percentage value. It's often compared the interest rate you might be receiving from a bank account on an annual basis. When looking at the dividend yield also factor in the dividend growth rate. You want to have an overall total-return potential made up of the yield and the annual growth rate for that dividend.

For growth dividend companies look for yields ranging from 2 to 4%. And with income dividend companies consider those yields that fall between 4 and 6%. As for the dividend growth rate, screen for growth companies in the 10 to 12% range for increasing the yield year over year and 6 to 10% for income companies. These parameters tend to be the sweet spots for both categories.

3. Compare the current dividend yield to the historical yield range.

Look for historically profitable companies that have a track record of rewarding shareholders with a portion of the profits through dividends. Check out the historical data for the company to see if the business has consistently raised their dividends over a 20 to 30-year period of time. Compare the current yield to the historical patterns noting those periods of time when the business had to operate in the midst of a poor economy. If the current yield is significantly higher than the historical trends, you may have a good buying opportunity. Recall that as stock prices drop, the current yield increases since it represents a greater percentage of the amount being potentially distributed.

As a side note, you shouldn't just focus on the current yield in assessing the merits of any dividend company. Current yields fluctuate with the stock price. To build in a margin of safety into the selection process focus on how the historical trends have impacted yield and returns.

4. Ensure that Free Cash Flow covers more than 50% of dividend payouts.

Similar to the payout ratio, look at the company's free cash flow for the quarter or the year in comparison to the quarterly or annual dividend payout. You want it to adequately cover the payment of the dividend to the shareholders. If the company doesn't have enough cash on hand to adequately deal with a temporary setback in the markets or business landscape, the dividend may be slashed.

Three additional rules to help you determine if the dividend yield may be too high are the following:

5. Avoid a stock if the dividend yield is 3% or more than the yield of typical dividend-paying stocks in its industry.

6. Avoid a stock if the yield is more than 4 times the overall market yield for the Dow Jones Industrial Average or the S&P 500.

7. Avoid a stock if the yield is more than twice its historical long-term average yield.

Much of this data can be obtained by checking resources like the Value Line Investment Survey and Barron's Market Laboratory. Keep in mind that extraordinary high yields don't result from the company increasing its dividends. It's usually the result of falling stock prices due to a systemic problem.

In general, you may wish to look for boring bank, insurance company and blue-chip stocks. Blue chip companies are those that have a national reputation for quality and reliability in good times and bad. The term blue chip came about from the game of poker in which blue chips have the highest value.

Covered Call Rules:

Another source of conservative income from stock positions that you own is by selling option contracts. This is a great way to tap into monthly or bi-monthly income coming from "renting" out your stocks. In exchange for the buyer of the options contract to have the right to purchase your shares at an agreed upon price, you (the seller of the contract) receive a cash premium up front for that privilege. Yippie skippy, I love getting cash up front.

Selling option contracts on stock that you own is a well-known income generation strategy that not only reduces your initial cost price for the stock, but it also builds in a margin of safety for preserving your capital. Also, when you're able to generate cash flow from multiple sources, such as options and dividends, this accelerates your wealth creation.

As a novice options trader, there's no reason to start out learning complex strategies. Some of the simplest most conservative strategies can be the most lucrative. Here are some general rules to keep in mind when options trading using covered calls.

8. Learn to use a variety of covered call option strategies, not just one.

As with any new endeavor, it's important to learn before you earn. Take the time to learn how to move into and out of the options market with a high degree of confidence. Although covered call writing is a conservative investment approach, you will need to be comfortable with the specialized vocabulary and a handful of strategies before trading. This means taking the time to paper trade for at least one month before committing any positions to this income generation approach.

Here's an important rule to keep in mind that's advocated by Lawrence McMillan author of "New Insights on Covered Call Writing".

9. Trade in accordance with your comfort level and psychological identity.

And as Michael Thomsett puts it:

> *"Using high-volatility stocks as a vehicle for producing current income from call writing is an appropriate strategy - as long as you can accept the*

> higher than average risks that go along with this strategy."

Each individual investor comes to the table with a different level of appetite for taking on risk. Most investment educators would caution novice investors to learn before they earn. As Robert Kiyosaki, author of "Rich Dad's Guide to Investing", so appropriately states:

> "It's not the investment that is risky, it's the investor."

He goes on to explain that skilled professionals can consistently make money in any market because they understand risk and account for it in their investment decisions.

Allan Ellman, the creator of "The Blue Collar Investor" subscription website recommends limiting your exposure to increased risk in the options market by looking for conservative returns.

It is stock price volatility that drives option pricing. The higher the price volatility, the more lucrative the option contract. The trade-off is that this puts you at greater risk of capital loss. Ellman and other conservative option traders recommend the following:

10. Look for monthly option returns of less than 4%.

This basic rule of thumb should keep most conservative option traders out of trouble and improve your chances of making money with options. As a side note, the sweet spot for consistent, successful monthly covered call trades tends to fall in the 2 to 3% range. This potentially translates into double digit returns on your stock holdings just from options premiums being deposited into your brokerage account.

11. Avoid trading covered calls in months with a quarterly earnings report.

Any report that can introduce uncertainty into the markets can be a catalyst for increased stock price volatility. When trading in the options market, higher levels of volatility translate into greater fluctuations in option valuations. Wild price swings can and do occur. To protect any covered call positions, you'll want to avoid scheduling any sell options for those months reporting quarterly earnings. It's best to sit on the sidelines for one month to see how the markets will react.

Guy Cohen, author of "Options Made Easy" suggests that one should only trade when the most obvious opportunities present themselves in the market and with a specific trade. Patience becomes the name of the game when selling covered calls.

Should you like to explore covered call options strategies in greater detail, I would recommend checking out the guide **"Cash Flow Stock Investing"**.

4

GROWTH INVESTING

A growth investing approach capitalizes on rising stock price appreciation whether it's due to an overall upswing in stock market sentiment, outstanding growth for a particular market sector or better than average growth in a specific stock. You're able to capitalize on above average stock price appreciation, thus increasing the velocity of your money. Put another way, you're able to increase the speed at which you're able to double your holdings over time.

James Cramer has often advocated in his books and TV appearances that as a do-it-yourself growth investor you need to start by following this basic rule:

1. Buy best-of-breed stocks that are market leaders.

In order to use any type of growth strategy, you'll want to focus your attention on those stocks having the greatest potential for rapid growth. Logic would dictate that those stocks having solid fundamentals and having positioned themselves as leaders in their respective industries, are the most likely to continue appreciating in price and value.

When using a momentum investing approach, professional trader Joe Terranova suggests following this basic rule:

2. Buy high with the intent to sell higher.

You'll often pay more up front for growth stocks having a lot of momentum behind them.

Mark Minervini, who won the 1997 US Investing Championship, actively buys high PE stocks, as this is one metric that shows where the momentum and growth is. When you analyze some of the fastest growing businesses over the past few years, you'll discover that they all traded at high PE's (Price to

Earnings ratios). This translates into making extensive returns when the company in question has solid business fundamentals.

Traditional money managers often believe PE's should be low. Minervini and Terranova often use a contrarian approach. However, it should be pointed out that both investors do their homework on the viability of the company along with the growth potential in the immediate economic climate.

To help you better assess those growth companies worthy of your investment dollar let's take a look at some of William O'Neil's growth investing rules. William O'Neil is the author of "How to Make Money in Stocks" and creator of the CAN SLIM investment system. Here are three of his most important growth rules to consider.

3. Look for 3 years of annual earnings in excess of 25%.

Sales is what drives growth in any business. When annual earnings grow in excess of 25% over a few years, you're seeing a rapidly expanding business. It may be due to a regional powerhouse company expanding nationally. It could also be the due to increased market share of a newly launched technology or development. Digging a little deeper into the company's business model should shed some additional insights into what is causing this phenomenal growth.

Look at the three-year growth rate to weed out 80% of the stocks in a given sector. You want to insist on annual earnings increases with recent quarterly earnings improvements. And don't be fooled into thinking you should buy low P/E ratio stocks.

4. Screen for an EPS growth rate in excess of 18% for the last 2-3 quarters.

As an investor, you're most concerned about how the company's earnings compare to the shares being held. Since you own a portion of the business, the EPS growth rate helps you assess whether your stake in the company is growing.

Always compare the stock's percentage increase in EPS for the quarter ending in December to the same December quarter a year earlier. You also don't want to turn completely negative on a company's earnings until you've seen a significant slowdown over at least two quarters. Some of the best businesses in the market can show signs of periodic slowdowns, especially those stocks that are tied to seasonal or economic sector rotations.

For example, companies in the oil sector can experience solid growth in the last and first quarters in the year due to increased winter demand for heating oil. However, with lower demand during the summer, these solid companies can experience a slight pullback in stock pricing.

You'll also see a similar profitability pattern emerge with defensive stocks during a recession. Defensive stocks are those businesses that provide goods and services that everyone needs no matter whether the economy is booming or sliding back. Healthcare and Consumer Staple sectors are subject to sector rotations during the course of a normal economic cycle.

5. Consider those stocks with a Return on Equity (ROE) in excess of 17%.

The Return on Equity ratio or return on net assets provides you with insight into how efficiently the company's management team is handling shareholder contributions. It's a measure of the profitability of a business in relation to stockholders' equity. A high ROE translates into a business model capable of returning high profits.

One technical indicator to consider in the mix of stock investment rules is the Relative Strength Index or RSI. It measures the magnitude and velocity of price movements in a particular stock. The RSI is plotted on a technical chart with a scale from 0 to 100. The scale has high and low levels marked at 80 and 20, respectively.

James O'Shaughnessy, in his book "What Works on Wall Street", says that:

> *"We find that relative strength is among the only pure growth factors that actually beats the market consistently, by a wide margin."*

6. Screen for stocks with an initial RSI between 50 and 80.

By considering those stocks showing signs of growth and momentum on their side, you're able to get into momentum plays earlier.

William O'Neil also has a rule for a stock's RSI. He avoids stocks with an RSI below 70, since these potential picks generally lag behind better-performing ones in the overall market. He looks for those rapid growers with an RSI in excess of 85. Just be cautious of your entry point into the market as the RSI approaches 100, as this typically signals that the stock may be oversold. Oversold stocks tend to return back closer to the mean when the big boys take profits off the table and wait for the next appropriate buy-in opportunity.

Which brings us to what investment icon Peter Lynch follows as a rule of thumb:

7. *The lower the PEG, the better.*

The PEG ratio is useful for comparing like businesses together. It represents the ratio between the Price-to-Earnings or PE multiple divided by the company's earnings growth rate. This is a good indicator of growth-at-a-reasonable price or what is known as GARP, which should not be confused with GORP, which is good old raisins and peanuts.

The PEG identifies growth stocks that are still selling at a good price. The lower the PEG the better, since you're getting more earnings growth for every dollar invested. Typically, fundamentally solid companies have PEG ratios of less than 1, whereas a PEG ratio over 2 is expensive.

5

MARKET TIMING

Despite what you may have read or heard about trying to time the stock market, there are certain periods of time that do tend to produce better results from a historical perspective than others. The argument that many investment gurus will make is that it is true that you won't be able to consistently time market tops and bottoms. No one has been able to do so.

However, when you focus on timing opportunities that are stock specific, you can take advantage of certain times of the week and year to gain a slight edge. Let's take a look at some of the timing rules to consider, starting with Warren Buffett's favorite rule.

1. *Be greedy, when others are fearful.*

What Buffett is referring to is that some of the best value investments can be made when the stock market is experiencing a major market correction from being oversold. As you know, the stock market doesn't travel upwards in a straights line. It tends to rise and fall, snaking its way upward.

Bob Farrell, who was the chief stock market analyst at Merrill Lynch says:

> *"The public buys the most at the top and the least at the bottom."*

As stock prices drop during these pullbacks, panic sets in. Many inexperienced investors fearing that the end is near, sell their holdings. As the sell-off momentum picks up steam, the stock prices of solid companies also drop as panic grips the overall market.

These precise moments can allow the contrarian investor to enter the market and pick up shares of stock trading below fair market value. In effect, you're able to purchase stock with a margin of safety built in.

Stock market corrections usually occur on average at least once or twice a year. Let me put this into perspective. Besides a major correction due to COVID-19 in March 2020 we've had five corrections since August 2019. These corrections provide the astute investor opportunities to acquire stock at below fair market value. This is why you should always have cash on hand in your stock investment account for these panic-driven opportunities, which brings us to what Warren Buffett, James Cramer and other investors tout.

2. Cash is for winners. Keep some aside for unanticipated opportunities.

It's okay to keep a portion of your investment portfolio in cash as long as it is being targeted for future opportunities. Not having a cash reserve limits your ability to take advantage of these market corrections when they transpire. And as the Jedi master Yoda says:

> *"Transpire they will."*

Piggybacking off of this advice is what James Cramer suggests doing.

3. *Don't buy major stock positions all at once.*

With online discount brokerage fees currently being so low, one can afford to purchase shares in blocks staggered throughout the week or month. By monitoring investor sentiment through various news sources and examining technical charts of the market as a whole along with the individual stocks, you can get a better feel for the market's mood.

You may be asking yourself why not use the automated investment approach of making stock purchases using a dollar cost averaging approach. Here's what many stock investing experts would suggest. If you have no interest in monitoring your stock investments, this may be an effective strategy to use as it forces you to make regular purchases over time. However, if you're considering following the sage advice of some of the successful investors showcased in this guide, you may wish to reconsider this option.

By investing on a specific monthly date, you're unable to take advantage of price fluctuations that do occur. As you're about to discover, there are certain times of the week and year that prove to be either more profitable or problematic.

Unfortunately, you're not able to adjust for these fluctuations with dollar-cost averaging. You may end up paying more for your positions than need be by using the alternative approach of being more patient and systematic.

Jeffrey and Yale Hirsch, producers of the "Stock Trader's Almanac", have identified historical patterns in the stock market that you can use to your advantage. Here's one of their key tips:

4. Try to place trades mid-week on Wednesday's.

According to their research, Wednesday's have produced the most gains since tracking this metric back in the 1990's. Mid-week doesn't have the same problems as the ends of the week.

Both Monday's and Friday's can show signs of increased volatility. This can translate into overpaying for a stock. By being more methodical in your approach you can sidestep these potential pitfalls.

As Joe Terranova points out in his book "Buy High Sell Higher":

5. *Avoid buying stock or call options on Monday's.*

Having worked professionally as a trading floor boss, he's experienced firsthand how volatile the markets can be on Monday's. Here's what he has to say:

> *"Whether traders love or hate their personal lives, the pros that move the market often come into the office on Mondays in a bad mood. Whatever the reason, there is always a flood of emotion coursing through the market on Mondays. Markets that are trading on emotions are not where you want to be. I make a point of never trading on Mondays."*

Emotions can be a huge part to your success as an investor. When you understand how emotionally charged the markets can be at certain times, you position yourself to better take advantage of these situations that most investors get caught up in.

6. *Avoid trading first thing in the morning.*

Markets tend to be more volatile at the opening bell. The big boys tend to take profits or solidify their positions in the morning when their traders are fresh, and the markets are emotionally charged.

Waiting until after the noon-hour lull in trading often produces more predictable and consistent buy opportunities. Also, look for sell opportunities at the end of the day if you're seeing rising stock prices on higher than normal volume. This situation signals that investors are confident in a particular stock.

7. *Avoid trading after any big announcement.*

Most savvy investors would suggest that you heed this advice when company earnings are being announced or when federal government economic reports are released. Earning reports can easily shift momentum patterns temporarily creating volatile trading scenarios. The same can be said of any major economic announcement by the federal government or news-breaking media reporting.

As James Cramer points out you should also:

> *"Wait 30 days after warnings."*

When you see multiple stock market analysts downgrading a particular stock, hold off investing in the equity until you see a definitive pattern in the stock's price movement. By giving the markets a month to readjust, you may be in a better situation to both verify the position's fundamentals and Mr. Market's take on the situation.

Investing champion Mark Minervini offers this sage advice:

8. Where's the exit? Avoid the emotional stop-loss.

You should determine at which point you'll exit any stock position before placing any trade. By focusing on the downside, you can mitigate any potential huge losses. He suggests setting up a series of stop loss scenarios for each of your positions, as follows:

1. Set a stop loss order on your stock position as soon as you've received confirmation for your buy order. You want to limit your loss. Determine how much you're prepared to lose and then set a stop loss. Many investor's use 5% as a starting point.
2. Protect your gains. Once the stock price climbs and is showing a decent profit, reset your stop loss so that it's near your breakeven point.
3. Protect you profits by using a trailing stop or

a back stop. You want to try to lock in your profits as the position moves up.

Incidentally, a stop loss is just a sell order you set up to be automatically executed when the current stock price triggers the sale of the stock. Stop losses can be set based on a fixed price, self-adjusting percentage loss as the stock price moves up and down, or a self-adjusting dollar value loss.

An emotional stop-loss is the point at which the loss of capital in your holding becomes too great to bear any longer, and you sell out of frustration. To win big in the stock market, you must not lose big. Use a series of stop loss scenarios to control risk.

Keep in mind that a 33 percent drop requires a 50 percent rise to break even. Hence, the importance of cutting your losses quickly.

6

MENTAL TRAINING

This final chapter ties all of the fundamental and technical rules of investing together. It's a crucial part to becoming the do-it-yourself investor you desire to become. How you envision the stock market as a whole and how you react emotionally to what is taking place in the markets impacts your buying and selling decisions. The challenge with investing is that the problems that arise are not in the market but in ourselves.

The stock market, for the most part, is a voting machine. Industries and specific stocks come into favor with Mr. Market and go out of favor when another opportunity shows potentially better promise. However, as investing legend Bob Farrell points out:

"Markets tend to return to the mean over time."

It's important to realize that the stock market over historically long periods of time in excess of 60 years trend upwards with an annual average growth rate around 10%. The temporary ups and downs of the market will try your patience, resolve and discipline. Let's see if we can sack the odds in our favor, by exploring the mental game of investing.

Denise Shull, the author of "Market Mind Games", which explores investment decision psychology offers this fundamental rule:

1. Look at trading as a physical game.

Athletes are able to achieve high-performance levels when they've finely tuned their bodies, attitudes and minds for competition. Shull argues that to be successful, investors need to take into account the sum total of their physical, mental and emotional energy available at any one time when placing a trade. She refers to this as your "psyche cap" or your total mental or psychological capital.

Your psyche cap can vary depending on factors affecting your life at any one given moment. With this in mind, you should not trade when you're sick or tired since your psyche cap will be at a low level. This could disrupt your edge in the markets. Trading when you're under the weather can result in investment portfolio losses.

It's important to consider working on all three aspects affecting your psyche cap. When you improve your physical state of being, this helps your mental ability, which in turn augments your ability to read the market and improves your overall results. Start by taking good care of your body with proper nutrition, regular physical activity and quality time for relaxation or reflection.

2. Treat your feelings as data. Learn to notice your different combinations of feelings when you place any trades.

Denise Shull in her ground-breaking book, quotes a recent scientific study in saying that:

"Contrary to the popular belief that feelings are generally bad for decision making, we found that individuals who experienced more intense feelings had higher decision-making performance..."

She went on to say that individuals who were better able to identify and distinguish among their current feelings achieved higher decision-making performance.

But hold on there, Randall. Others are saying the exact opposite. As Bob Farrell says:

"Our emotions can get the better of us."

Or as Vanguard Investment Advisor John Bogle tells investors:

"Eliminate emotion from your investment program. Have rational expectations for future returns and avoid changing those expectations in response to the ephemeral noise coming from Wall Street."

Now, the question becomes: Should you ignore or embrace your emotions?

Shull feels that emotions provide us with valuable insights into how we invest. So, if you decide to use your emotions as a tool, how do you train your emotions to serve your needs better? Shull believes that you need to get to know your emotions, not completely subvert them.

First, anticipate how your body will react when you make an investment decision. She then says to notice which feelings arise. And finally take a second to name your feeling and jot it down in some sort of trading journal or diary. I usually record my reactions in my day planner. Was I feeling anger, fear, disgust, sadness or pleasure? This has helped me identify weaknesses in my trading.

As legendary portfolio manager Peter Lynch states:

> "The most important organ is the stomach, not the brain."

That gut feeling you're developing should hopefully guide you in your decision-making process. The more conscious you become of your feelings, the faster you'll be able to use this information about yourself in risk management and decision-making. Your goal is to shift your emotions towards the more stable ground of contentment, rather than fear or euphoria. This effectively translates into making more confident decisions.

Remember that Mr. Market doesn't care about feelings of euphoria or panic. Mr. Market doesn't attach an emotional label to any particular situation unfolding in the stock market. We are wrong when are euphoric about stocks going up. And we are wrong when we beat ourselves up when they go down. It's you, the investor, who must learn to cope with non-productive emotions and strive to foster feelings of confidence and patience.

Emotions are the #1 factor into accounting for trading mistakes. As Mark Douglas points out in his book "Trading in the Zone":

> *"It's attitudes and beliefs about being wrong, losing money and the tendency to become reckless, when you're feeling good, that causes most losses - not technique or market knowledge."*

This brings us to another key element of your mental training. Mark Douglas advocates spending time developing the mental aspect to your investing and not just knowledge about the stock investment approaches and strategies.

3. Create a winning mindset that gives you an edge in the markets.

Your objective should be to slowly adjust your attitude about investing so you can move effortlessly in and out of opportunities without fear. You need to develop a system that doesn't allow you to become reckless, nor is it fuelled by non-productive emotions. In doing so, you dramatically increase your chances of success.

Your edge in the markets is nothing more than an indication of a higher probability of one thing happening over another. Developing that edge starts with identifying those emotions that surface when making investment decisions. The next step is to change your beliefs by looking at the market in a different light.

The stock market is made up of institutional and individual investors all of which come with a mixed bag of emotions. Since the stock market is driven by shifts in investor moods, it helps to think of investing in a different light. Try to look at each investment opportunity through the eyes of all of the other investors. How do you think they would react to the unfolding situation? It's not how good you think you are that counts, it's how good you are in comparison to your competitors.

Learn to think about how the future will play out in the other investor's minds. When you shift to thinking socially about how the markets will react, you place yourself in the correct mindset to make better quality investment decisions.

4. Have a process. Embrace that process.

Investment champion Mark Minervini has developed his edge in the markets by sticking to a set of rules he clings to closely to his heart, like a sacred religious artifact. He is disciplined and focused on process. Mark strives to perfect his craft knowing that positive results follow the successful execution of his plan. The mistakes he makes are viewed as valuable feedback in order to learn how to perfect his investment system.

Keep in mind that hope is not an investment plan. Being hopeful is helpful; however, in investing it's much better to be objective and realistic. Begin by asserting your role as an expert on your own needs. Take the time to determine which investment approaches you want to explore that'll help you achieve your specific goals down the road.

Are you looking at 40 years or 15 years ahead of you in the investment arena? What do you want your investments to fund in the future? How much time are you willing to commit to the investment process? Which strategies and approaches resonate with you the most?

Keep in mind that "time" is the single-most powerful factor in any investment plan. The length of time investments will be held and the period of time your investments will be measured and judged, transforms investments from least attractive to most attractive.

Minervini's sentiments about following a specific investment process are echoed in what Marcel Link, author of "High Probability Trading" says about stock investing, namely:

"Follow a trading plan."

Following a plan, or put another way, following a pre-defined set of rules for:

- selecting wonderful stocks,
- purchasing shares when the timing is appropriate,
- protecting your investment capital with call options or stop loss orders,
- optimizing your income streams from dividends and covered call premiums and
- adhering to specific exit or sell criteria,

All of these factors increase your edge in the markets. This slight advantage gained is just enough to realize more profitable positions than unprofitable over time.

In developing your investment plan consider implementing these key elements:

- What "buy" trigger criteria will you adhere to?
- How will you mitigate risk?
- How and when will you lock in your profits?
- How will you determine your position size for your holdings?

In order to better prepare for these key elements, create a series of "what if" scenarios and responses. This allows you to develop contingency strategies that'll avert any disasters.

James Cramer is known for this insightful rule.

5. Bulls and Bears make money, pigs get slaughtered.

Greed in investing is a disease that'll send you to the poorhouse. If you want to consistently generate returns, you must ignore the temptations of high returns. Don't be a stock market pig. Your goal as an investor is to optimize your returns, not to maximize them.

Also, keep in mind that hope is never a good trading strategy. As James Cramer likes to say:

> "Never subsidize losers with winners."

In other words, don't cash out of winning positions in order to continue pumping money into losing positions in the hope that things will turn around.

You actually want to develop the discipline to hold onto your winners and quickly dispose of your losers. It's psychologically challenging to cut your losses when you should. However, capital preservation should be foremost on your mind when you invest in any market.

6. Beware of the Wall Street investo-tainment hype.

Buying on tips, rumors, and other news events, stories, or opinions you hear from supposed market experts on TV or the social media is a recipe for disaster. Just because a famous investment guru says it's so, doesn't mean that it is. Trust your system and your good judgement.

As Warren Buffett so infamously stated:

"Most news is noise, not news."

You should never make impulsive decisions. Do your homework first to see if the numbers pan out. Then, make an educated decision based on those pre-defined rules you've adopted for your style of investing. Rules are meaningless without discipline.

Stick to your investment philosophy and your analytical process as to when to buy and sell equities. Try to follow it with patience and discipline.

As Bob Farrell puts it:

"Fear and greed are stronger than long-term resolve."

When these two emotions are coursing through the stock market, your resolve may be tested, especially with those holdings you would like to hang onto long-term. As investors, we tend to overreact to bad news and to good news.

We grin from ear to ear when our stock go up and curse and frown when they go down. And our feelings tend to get stronger and stronger the more - and the faster - the stock prices rise or fall. This is why having a trading plan with pre-defined rules will keep you out of emotionally troublesome scenarios.

Much of the learning involved in investing is experience-based. In fact, the most valuable form of learning about investing is experience-based. You'll have extreme experiences where you'll find out more about yourself in good times and bad. If you would like to become a brilliant investor learn from those terrible experiences and step back up to the plate to apply what you've learned.

In closing, I hope that these rules and insights have empowered you to become a better, well-rounded investor. As you may have surmised, this guide has walked you through various investment approaches that follow a natural progression from being a more passive investor with a long-term time horizon to one who embraces the challenge of being more actively involved in the investment process.

Whatever philosophical investment approach you decide to take, try to incorporate at least some of these rules into your model. As you can see, they have served many respected investors and educators well.

Should you like to learn more about the power of cash flow stock investing, then I encourage you to pick up a copy of "**Cash Flow Stock Investing**" on Amazon. Explore more of what this in-depth resource has to offer.

Learn how to make money in all market conditions. Generate consistent, monthly streams of income from stocks you own and reach your financial goals that much faster.

As Mark Douglas points out:

"Every moment in the market is unique."

There are always great investment opportunities presenting themselves on a regular basis. No need to fear losing out on the next best thing to sliced bread. However, you do want to position yourself in any investment opportunity with a set of pre-defined rules that'll give you the confidence to reach your full potential as an investor.

I hope that these insights have given you some concrete rules you can use to your advantage in the future. Should you like to explore stock investing approaches in greater detail, please check out the following free resources:

Stock Investing Tool Kit

Get $29 Worth of Investment Research for Free

To get your bonuses, go to: http://tiny.cc/stock-investing

BIOGRAPHIES:

Laura Adams:

Adams is a personal finance and small business expert, who grew up in South Carolina. She has an MBS from the University of Florida. Adams is an award-winning author, media spokesperson and renowned speaker. Since 2013, she has completed more than 2,500 interviews about financial literacy. Her claim to fame is in making complex finance topics easy to understand. She is the author of several books: Money-Smart Solopreneur, Debt-Free Blueprint and Money Girl's Smart Moves to Grow Rich.

Biographies:

John "Jack" Bogle:

Bogle was an American investor, business magnate and philanthropist, who grew up in Montclair, New Jersey. He is credited with creating the first Index Fund when he founded The Vanguard Group. Bogle is most famous for his books Stay the Course, The Clash of the Cultures, Enough, and The Little Book of Common Sense Investing.

Warren Buffett:

Buffett is an iconic American investor and the chairman and CEO of Berkshire Hathaway. He's looked upon as being one of the most successful investors in the world. He's also one of the pioneers of value investing. Buffett was born in Omaha, Nebraska and graduated from the Columbia School of Business. Many books have been written about Buffett; of note are Warren Buffett on Business, The Snowball, and The Warren Buffett Portfolio.

Charles Carlson:

Carlson is a certified financial advisor who attended the University of Chicago. He is the CEO of Horizon

Publishing and Horizon Investment Services, which offers money management services. Carlson has published 8 books; of note are Buying Stocks without a Broker, The Little Book of Big Dividends, and Winning with the DOW's Losers. He's a big advocate of generating income through dividend stocks.

James Cramer:

Cramer is an American television personality and flamboyant host of Mad Money on CNBC. Born in Wyndmoor, Pennsylvania, he attended both Harvard Law School and Harvard University. Cramer is a former hedge fund manager and is the co-founder of TheStreet.com. He has several books to his credit, such as Get Rich Carefully, Getting Back to Even, Mad Money and Real Money.

MJ DeMarco:

DeMarco is a successful entrepreneur and business author. His claim to fame is in investing $900 into an online limousine business that turned into a multimillion-dollar company several years later. After the sale of the company, he wrote the international bestseller The Millionaire Fastlane and recently released his second entrepreneurship book called Unscripted.

Mark Douglas:

Douglas was a well-known trading educator. He's best known for his seminal book Trading in the Zone, which is about the psychology of making money in the stock market. He also wrote The Disciplined Trader a book aimed to help stock and future traders to achieve the psychological trading discipline needed to trade. Douglas was also the president of the trading firm Trading Behavior Dynamics.

Allan Ellman:

Former dentist turned covered call guru, Ellman is the President of The Blue Collar Investor corporation. Ellman is an educator foremost with countless books and DVD courses in the stock investing arena to his credit. He is best known for his books Cashing in on Covered Calls, Exit Strategies for Covered Calls, Stock Investing for Students and Selling Cash-Secured Puts.

Bob Farrell:

Farrell was the chief stock market analyst and senior investment advisor at Merrill Lynch for a period of 45 years. He joined the company back in 1957. He's well known as a technical analyst in recognizing the importance of data and patterns. Farrell is best known for his 10 trusty rules for investing.

Jeffrey and Yale Hirsch:

Yale created the Stock Trader's Almanac back in 1967. It was instrumental in popularizing trading strategies that were based on historical data, cycles and patterns. Jeffrey joined the organization as a market analyst and historian. Both the annual almanac and digital subscription service explain how investors can beat the market.

Benjamin Graham:

British-born economist, professor and investor, Benjamin Graham is known as the godfather of value investing. He's best known for his blockbuster stock investment guide The Intelligent Investor, which was released in 1949. Warren Buffett attributes much of his early success to Graham.

Biographies:

Marcel Link:

Link has been a professional trader since 1987. He has documented much of his trading experience in his books. Link is best known for his two books: High-Probability Trading and Trading without Gambling.

Peter Lynch:

Lynch was a legendary mutual fund manager of the Magellan Fund at Fidelity Investments, where he consistently averaged returns more than double the S&P 500. Born in Newton, Massachusetts, he attended both Boston College and Wharton School of the University of Pennsylvania. He is best known for his books One Up on Wall Street and Beating the Street.

Burton Malkiel:

Malkiel is an American economist and writer, who hails from Boston, Massachusetts. He's a graduate of the Harvard Business School. His classic book A Random Walk Down Wall Street was first published in 1973. He's a big proponent of the efficient-market hypothesis and advocates buying and holding index funds as the most effective portfolio management strategy.

Lawrence G. McMillan:

Working as a proprietary trader at two major brokerage houses, McMillan has been directly involved in both options trading and education. He is best known for his book Options: A Strategic Investment.

Mark Minervini:

Minervini won the 1997 U.S. Investing Championship using a long-only stock portfolio to win the real-money investment derby with a 155% annual return, a performance that was nearly double his nearest competitor. He's the author of Trade Like a Stock Market Wizard and Think and Trade Like a Champion. Minervini educates traders about his SEPA® methodology through Minervini Private Access, which is an online trading platform.

Paul Mladjenovic:

Mladjenovic is a well-known certified financial planner and investing consultant. He has several books to his credit, such as Stock Investing for Dummies, Precious Metals Investing for Dummies, and Micro-Entrepreneurship for Dummies. All of these books are easy to digest. He's also the author of the Prosperity Alert newsletter.

James O'Shaughnessy:

O'Shaughnessy grew up in Saint Paul, Minnesota where he developed a penchant for quantitative research in the stock market. He is credited for starting his own mutual funds and currently runs O'Shaughnessy Asset Management. He is the author of What Works on Wall Street, How to Retire Rich, and Predicting the Markets of Tomorrow.

Steve Smith:

Smith has over 30 years of investment experience, primarily in the options arena. He was a member of the Chicago Board of Trade and The Chicago Board Options Exchange for six years. Smith has been a major contributor to OptionAlert, OptionSmith, and Option Sensei newsletters. He shows stock investors the right way to use options to reduce risk and increase returns.

Joe Terranova:

Terranova is the chief market strategist for Virtus Investment Partners. Prior to that he spent 18 years as a trading floor boss in which he managed more than 300 traders. He's the author of Buy High, Sell Higher. Terranova is known for his risk management skills, which are shared in his book.

Michael C. Thomsett:

Thomsett is a prolific writer having published over 70 stock investing books, including Bloomberg Visual Guide to Candlestick Charting, Getting Started in Options, Options Trading for the Conservative Investor and Trading with Candlesticks. He has been writing professionally since 1978 and lives in Nashville, Tennessee.

Phil Town:

Town is an American Investor, motivational speaker and author of two books Rule #1 and Payback Time. Born in Portland, Oregon, Town went from becoming a rafting tour guide in Arizona to a successful seven-figure stock investor in five years. He has developed a value investing approach that centers around four key principles: Meaning, Moat, Management and Margin of Safety.

Denise Shull:

Shull holds a master's degree from The University of Chicago. She is a high-performance coach who works with hedge fund managers and professional athletes. Shull spent over a decade working as a short-term technical trader. She is the founder of The ReThink Group. She is also the author of Market Mind Games.

36 RESOURCES TO EXPLORE

Here is a list of the majority of the resources that I've used over the years to help me become a better investor. Some of these are classic guides that have stood the test of time. Should something tickle your fancy, check out those topics that may be of interest.

A Random Walk Down Wall Street: The Time-Tested Strategy for Successful Investing by Burton Malkiel

Publisher: W. W. Norton & Company (2020)

Paperback: 480 pages

All About Market Indicators: The Easy Way to Get Started by Michael Sincere Publisher: McGraw Hill (2011)

Paperback: 217 pages

Beating the Street: by Peter Lynch

Publisher: Simon & Schuster (1993)

Hardcover: 318 pages

Buy and Hedge: The 5 Iron Rules for Investing Over the Long Term by Jay Pestrichelli & Wayne Ferbert

Publisher: FT Press (2012)

Hardcover: 289 pages

Buy High Sell Higher: Why Buy-AND-Hold Is Dead & Other Investing Lessons from CNBC's "The Liquidator" by Joe Terranova

Publisher: Business Plus (2012)

Hardcover: 261 pages

Cash Flow Stock Investing by Randall Stewart

Publisher: Stewart Edge Publishing (2018)

Paperback: 276 pages

Cashing in on Covered Calls by Alan Ellman

Publisher: SAMR Productions (2007)

Paperback: 392 pages

DNA of Success by Jack Zufelt

Publisher: Z Publishing (2003)

Paperback: 208 pages

Exit Strategies for Covered Calls by Alan Ellman

Publisher: Wheatmark (2009)

Paperback: 178 pages

Getting Back to Even: Your Personal Economic Recovery Plan by James J. Cramer

Publisher: Simon & Schuster (2009)

Hardcover: 352 pages

Getting Started in Options by Michael Thomsett

Publisher: John Wiley & Sons (2007)

Paperback: 383 pages

High Probability Trading by Marcel Link

Publisher: McGraw Hill (2003)

Hardcover: 393 pages

How to Make Money in Stocks by William O'Neil

Publisher: McGraw Hill (2009)

Paperback: 464 pages

Intelligent Investor: The Definitive Book on Value Investing by Benjamin Graham, et al.

Publisher: Harper Business (2006)

Paperback: 640 pages

Little Book of Big Dividends: A Safe Formula for Guaranteed Returns by Charles B. Carlson

Publisher: John Wiley & Sons (2010)

Hardcover: 174 pages

Little Book of Common Sense Investing by John Bogle

Publisher: Wiley (2017)

Paperback: 304 pages

Market Mind Games by Denise Shull

Publisher: McGraw-Hill (2011)

Hardcover: 288 pages

Millionaire Fastlane by MJ DeMarco

Publisher: Viperion (2011)

Paperback: 322 pages

Millionaire Maker: Act, Think, and Make Money the Way the Wealthy Do by Loral Langemeier

Publisher: McGraw-Hill (2005)

Hardcover: 240 pages

Millionaire Next Door: The Surprising Secrets of America's Wealthy by Thomas Stanley & William Danko

Publisher: Taylor Trade Publishing (2010)

Paperback: 272 pages

Money Girl's Smart Moves to Grow Rich (Quick & Dirty Tips) by Laura Adams

Publisher: St. Martin's Griffin (2010)

Paperback: 254 pages

New Insights on Covered Call Writing by Richard Lehman & Lawrence McMillan

Publisher: Bloomberg Press (2003)

Hardcover: 240 pages

Options Made Easy: Your Guide to Profitable Trading by Guy Cohen

Publisher: FT Press (2005)

Hardcover: 335 pages

Options Trading for the Conservative Investor: Increasing Profits without Increasing Risk by Michael C. Thomsett

Publisher: Prentice Hall (2005)

Paperback: 255 pages

Power Curve by Scott Kyle

Publisher: Nautilus Press (2009)

Hardcover: 256 pages

Power of Focus by Jack Canfield, Mark Victor Hansen and Les Hewitt

Publisher: HCI (2000)

Paperback: 310 pages

Rich Dad's Guide to Investing by Robert Kiyosaki

Publisher: Time Warner Books (2000)

Paperback: 403 pages

Rule #1: The Simple Strategy for Successful Investing in Only 15 Minutes a Week by Phil Town

Publisher: Three Rivers Press (2007)

Paperback: 330 pages

Secrets of the Millionaire Mind by T. Harv Eker

Publisher: Harper Business (2005)

Hardcover: 224 pages

Stock Trader's Almanac by Jeffrey Hirsch & Yale Hirsch

Publisher: John Wiley & Sons

Hardcover: 192 pages

Succeed: How We Can Reach Our Goals by Dr. Heidi Grant Halverson

Publisher: Hudson Street Press (2010)

Hardcover: 288 pages

Trade Like a Stock Market Wizard by Mark Minervini

Publisher: McGraw-Hill Education (2013)

Hardcover: 352 pages

Trading in the Zone by Mark Douglas

Publisher: Prentice Hall Press (January 1, 2001)

Hardcover: 240 pages

Unfair Advantage: The Power of Financial Education by Robert Kiyosaki

Publisher: Plata Publishing (2011)

Paperback: 275 pages

Ultimate Dividend Playbook by Josh Peters

Publisher: John Wiley & Sons (2008)

Hardcover: 352 pages

What Works on Wall Street: The Classic Guide to the Best-Performing Investment Strategies of All Time by James P. O'Shaughnessy

Publisher: McGraw Hill (2012)

Hardcover: 681 pages

∾